MYTHOLOGY
AROUND THE WORLD

GREEK
MYTHS

by Eric Braun

Consultant:
Laurel Bowman, PhD
Assistant Professor and Graduate Advisor
Greek and Roman Studies
University of Victoria

CAPSTONE PRESS
a capstone imprint

Fact Finders Books are published by Capstone Press,
1710 Roe Crest Drive, North Mankato, Minnesota 56003
www.mycapstone.com

Library of Congress Cataloging-in-Publication Data
Names: Braun, Eric, 1971– author.
Title: Greek Myths / by Eric Braun.
Description: North Mankato: Capstone Press, 2019. |
Series: Fact Finders: Mythology Around the World
Identifiers: LCCN 2018006063| ISBN 9781515796060 (library binding) |
ISBN 9781515796206 (paperback)
Subjects: LCSH: Mythology, Greek—Juvenile literature.
Classification: LCC BL783 .B735 2018 | DDC 292.1/3—dc23
LC record available at https://lccn.loc.gov/2018006063

Editorial Credits
Editor: Jennifer Huston
Production Artist: Kazuko Collins
Designer: Russell Griesmer
Media Researcher: Morgan Walters
Production specialist: Kathy McColley

Photo Credits: Alamy: Heritage Image Partnership Ltd, 23; Bridgeman Images: Biagio Manfredi/
De Agostini Picture Library/A. Dagli Orti, 28, Brock, Charles Edmund, 19; Depositphotos:
vukkostic91, 9; Getty Images: DEA/A. DAGLI ORTI, 22, DEA/A. DE GREGORIO, 12, Kurt Miller/
Stocktrek Images, Cover; iStockphoto: Mlenny, 5; Newscom: akg-images/Peter Connolly, 17, 27,
Album/Oronoz, 13, Fine Art Images Heritage Images, 21, 24, The Print Collector Heritage Images, 6,
World History Archive, 15; Shutterstock: Anastasios71, 7, Cristiana Apostol, 29, G.roman, (lightning)
1, cover, Lukasz Szwaj, (paper texture) design element throughout, Madredus, (grunge) design
element throughout, MatiasDelCarmine, 10, 11, photocell, (plate) design element throughout,
RaZZeRs, (flare) 1, cover, Suchkov Nikolay, (pattern) design element, T.SALAMATIK, (rain texture)
design element throughout

Printed and bound in the USA.
PA021

TABLE OF CONTENTS

CHAPTER 1
The Culture of Ancient Greece 4

CHAPTER 2
The Greek Gods. 8

CHAPTER 3
The Stories 12

CHAPTER 4
The Trojan War 18

Glossary 30

Read More 31

Internet Sites 31

Critical Thinking Questions 31

Index 32

CHAPTER I

THE CULTURE OF ANCIENT GREECE

Imagine you lived thousands of years ago, before phones, electricity, or cars. The area where you live is made up of mountains, sea, and islands. That makes it difficult to meet people outside your own community. That's what it was like in ancient Greece. The people of these **city-states** shared a language, but they were mostly independent and **isolated**.

One thing the ancient Greeks shared was religion. Although the city-states were independent, many people worshipped the same gods and goddesses. They told the same stories, or myths, about them. They honored the gods in similar ways. Temples were plentiful and many religious ceremonies were held there.

INFLUENTIAL CULTURE

Most of Greece's power was centered in the city-state of Athens. Around 508 BC, the Greeks formed a new kind of government called **democracy**. In a democracy, citizens get to choose their leaders. Democracy is one of the ancient Greeks' most important contributions to the world.

city-state—a self-governing town and its surrounding territory

isolate—the condition of being alone

democracy—a form of government in which the citizens can choose their leaders and make decisions by voting

The Acropolis of Athens

The Acropolis was the most important place in Athens. The Greeks held festivals and other important events there. In the mid-400s BC, the ruler Pericles started a program to beautify Athens. During this time, many temples were built on the Acropolis, including the Parthenon. This was the temple of Athena, the warrior goddess for whom Athens was named. Although it was constructed nearly 2,500 years ago, the Parthenon still stands today.

Athens was also a center for art and culture. It was there that the world-famous Acropolis of Athens was built. An acropolis was a **fortified** mini-city built on a hill. Most city-states had an acropolis where citizens could go if under attack.

fortify—to construct walls or buildings to be used for military defenses

Intellectual Advancements

The ancient Greeks made many important discoveries in areas such as medicine, philosophy, math, astronomy, and engineering. Scientist Hippocrates is considered the father of modern medicine. Plato wrote important works in philosophy that are still studied today. Great thinkers such as Euclid and Pythagoras did important work in math and geometry.

Literature and theater were also important to the ancient Greeks. Greek playwrights wrote tragedies and comedies, inspiring works that are still performed today. During the mid-700s BC, Homer wrote his **epic poems** *The Iliad* and *The Odyssey*. *The Iliad* tells of the Trojan War. *The Odyssey* describes the journey home of the Greek hero Odysseus after the Trojan War.

Ancient Greek poet Homer is believed to have lived in the 8th century BC.

Millions of people visit the Parthenon every year.

Greek buildings and sculptures were simple but beautiful. The Greek styles of **architecture** are still seen in many buildings constructed in modern times.

TO HONOR THE GODS

In all these art forms, the importance of the Greek gods is clear. Gods were honored in plays, sculptures, and temples. The ancient Greeks believed the gods were always near. They also believed that the gods influenced what went on in their daily lives.

epic poem—a long story or poem about heroic adventures and great battles
architecture—the design of buildings

CHAPTER 2

THE GREEK GODS

The ancient Greeks told many stories, or myths, about how the world was created. The best-known story came from the poet Hesiod. According to him, in the beginning there was only an area of dark silence known as Chaos. Over time, Uranus, Gaea, and Tartarus sprang from Chaos. According to Greek tradition, Uranus represented the sky, Gaea was the earth, and Tartarus was the Underworld.

Uranus and Gaea were the parents of the first **immortal** beings, the **Titans**. Uranus hated his children and forced them to live in the Underworld. One of the Titans, Cronus, eventually defeated Uranus. After that, Cronus and the Titans ruled the world. But Uranus told Cronus that someday one of his children would defeat him, and then they would rule the world.

Cronus didn't want any of his children to defeat him. So whenever his wife, Rhea, gave birth to a child, Cronus swallowed it. He swallowed his first five children—Hades, Demeter, Hera, Hestia, and Poseidon. But when Zeus was born, Rhea secretly gave Cronus a stone to swallow instead of the baby. Then she hid Zeus from her husband.

immortal—able to live forever
Titan—a family of giants in Greek mythology born of Uranus and Gaea and ruling the earth until overthrown by the Olympian gods
trident—a long spear with three sharp points at its end

When Zeus was grown, he tricked Cronus into drinking a potion. Drinking it made him throw up all of the children he'd swallowed. The children were alive, full-grown, and unhurt. This started a war between the Titans and Zeus and his siblings. After 10 years of fighting, Zeus and his siblings conquered the Titans and sent Cronus to the Underworld. Zeus and his siblings took their place at the top of Mount Olympus and ruled the world from there.

During a war that lasted 10 years, Poseidon, Zeus, and Hades battled Cronus. Here, Poseidon (left) aims his three-pronged **trident** at the giant Cronus (center).

Over time, more gods and goddesses were born. They were immortal, and each had special skills or powers and ruled a certain part of life. Here are some of the main gods and goddesses of ancient Greece:

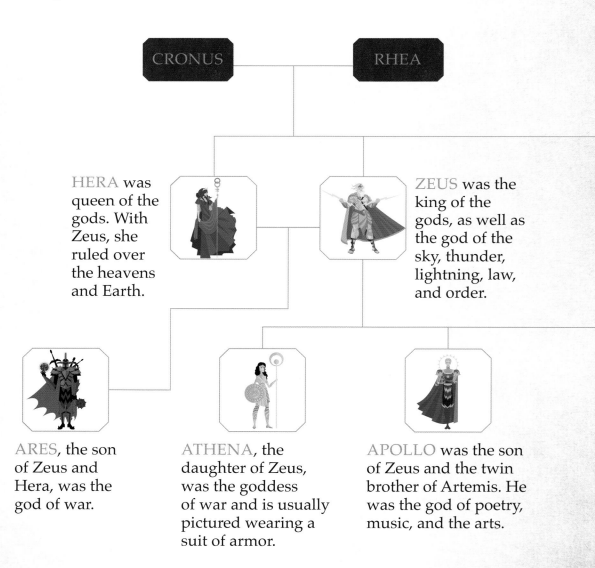

CRONUS ── **RHEA**

HERA was queen of the gods. With Zeus, she ruled over the heavens and Earth.

ZEUS was the king of the gods, as well as the god of the sky, thunder, lightning, law, and order.

ARES, the son of Zeus and Hera, was the god of war.

ATHENA, the daughter of Zeus, was the goddess of war and is usually pictured wearing a suit of armor.

APOLLO was the son of Zeus and the twin brother of Artemis. He was the god of poetry, music, and the arts.

The Birth of Athena

When Zeus heard that one of his children would become more powerful than him, he decided to do something to prevent it. When his wife Metis became pregnant, he swallowed her. The unborn child grew inside Zeus' head.

When Zeus started complaining of terrible headaches, he had someone split his head open with an ax. Because he was immortal, this didn't kill him. When Zeus' head was opened, his daughter Athena came out. She was full-grown and wearing a suit of armor.

 POSEIDON was Zeus' brother and the god of the sea and earthquakes.

 HADES was Zeus' brother and god of the Underworld, where he lived.

 ARTEMIS was the goddess of the hunt. Her arrows could kill instantly and without pain.

 APHRODITE, the goddess of love and beauty, had the power to make anyone fall in love. Her most powerful weapon was a magical belt that made her irresistible to all who saw her.

CHAPTER 3

THE STORIES

The myths helped the ancient Greeks make sense of an uncertain world. These stories explained how the world began, the seasons, and natural disasters, such as earthquakes and volcanic eruptions. But the gods sometimes caused trouble for humans.

MANKIND GETS FIRE

The Titan Prometheus had not taken sides during the war between the Titans and Zeus and his siblings. So after the war, the Olympian gods allowed him to live freely in the world. But Prometheus did not like the gods who had conquered his brothers and sisters. He especially disliked Zeus.

DID YOU KNOW?

Apollo was the god of sun and light. According to the Greeks, every day Apollo drove a golden chariot that pulled the sun across the sky.

In one story, Prometheus created mankind (or humans) out of mud. Zeus told Prometheus he could give mankind some gifts, but he could not give them fire. But Prometheus loved mankind. He knew that mankind needed fire to cook, stay warm, and create things. So Prometheus lit a torch from the fire of the gods and gave it to mankind. With fire, mankind began to build great cities.

Prometheus took fire from the gods and gave it to mankind.

Zeus was furious. To punish Prometheus, Zeus had him tied to a large rock. Every day Zeus sent an eagle to peck out Prometheus' liver and eat it. But because Prometheus was immortal, the liver grew back again each night. Every day the eagle returned to peck it out. Prometheus was eventually released from his punishment.

Pandora's Box

Zeus was not only angry with Prometheus, he was also upset that mankind was advancing with the help of fire. Zeus thought humans were too powerful, so he came up with a plan to weaken them. At the time, all humans were men, so Zeus had Hephaestus create the first woman. Her name was Pandora.

Zeus gave Pandora a box and, according to some stories, he told her she should never open it. But Pandora was curious about the box, so she opened it. The box contained disease, pain, poverty, jealousy, sadness, and death. She quickly closed the box, but it was too late. By opening the box, she had released into the world all the difficulties of human life. The only thing left in the box was hope.

Did You Know?

Today people use the expression "opening up Pandora's box" to describe a bad situation that is better left alone. It's something that looks harmless, but if not left alone could cause bad things to happen.

Despite Zeus' warning, Pandora opened the box he gave her.

The 12 Labors of Heracles

Some of the most important figures in Greek mythology were not gods but heroes. Heracles was one such hero. Although Zeus was Heracles' father, his mother was human, so Heracles was human too. Heracles had super-human strength, but he was quick-tempered and often acted before thinking things through.

Hera hated Heracles because he was the son of Zeus and another woman. She tried many times to have him killed. After Heracles was married and had a family, Hera sent Lyssa, the goddess of madness, to drive him mad.

In a state of madness, Heracles killed his wife and children. When he realized what he had done, he was filled with sadness. He prayed to Apollo to ask how he could make up for his terrible actions. Heracles was told that his punishment was to become a slave to a local king.

The king came up with 12 tasks that Heracles had to perform. Each of the labors was nearly impossible to complete. But Heracles completed them all. When he died several years later, Athena took him to Mount Olympus and brought him back to life. He remained there forever with the gods.

One of Heracles' 12 labors was to slay the Hydra. Whenever one of this serpent's nine heads was cut off, two new ones grew back. After Heracles cut off the heads, his nephew burned the stumps before new ones could grow.

CHAPTER 4

THE TROJAN WAR

The Trojan War was the last great battle of Greek mythology. Scholars now believe that the city of Troy was real. They also think that the story of the Trojan War may have been based partly on historical fact. But the stories and the role of the gods grew bigger over time.

The story begins when Zeus decided that there were too many humans on Earth. Zeus came up with a plan to reduce the number of humans through war. Troy was a wealthy, powerful city ruled by King Priam. But it was **foretold** that one of Priam's sons would bring about the fall of the city. So when Priam's son Paris was born, he was left in the woods to die. But the boy lived.

WHO'S THE FAIREST OF ALL?

Years later three goddesses were arguing over who was the most beautiful. Hera, Athena, and Aphrodite asked Zeus to decide, but he sent them to Paris, who was then a young man. Each of the three goddesses offered Paris gifts if he would choose her. Hera promised to make him a rich and powerful ruler. Athena promised him wisdom and success in battle. Aphrodite promised him the most beautiful human woman in the world, Helen of Sparta.

foretell—to predict something that will happen in the future

As Hera and Athena watched, Aphrodite promised to give Paris the most beautiful woman in the world.

Paris chose Aphrodite and journeyed to Sparta. While Helen's husband, King Menelaus, was away, Paris kidnapped her and brought her back to Troy. When Menelaus found out, he gathered a group of warriors to attack Troy and bring Helen back.

A great war broke out between the people of Troy (the Trojans) and the Spartans (the Greeks). Odysseus, Achilles, and Menelaus' brother, Agamemnon, were some of the Greeks' greatest warriors. Achilles was nearly immortal except for a spot on his heel. The Trojans also had great heroes, including Hector and Aeneas.

A LONG WAR

The Trojan War lasted for 10 years. The gods took sides in the war and used their powers to affect its outcome. Apollo, Artemis, and Aphrodite helped the Trojans. Athena, Hera, and Poseidon sided with the Greeks.

Many of the warriors also argued and fought amongst themselves. Near the end of the war, Agamemnon and Achilles had a bitter quarrel. Furious after the argument, the mighty Achilles quit the war.

Paris took Helen from Sparta and brought her to Troy.

Finally it was decided that Menelaus and Paris would fight each other to decide the outcome of the war. But when Paris started to lose, Aphrodite whisked him away and hid him. Then the war resumed.

DID YOU KNOW?

When Achilles was born, his mother, Thetis, tried to make him immortal by dipping him into the River Styx. The river was said to have magical powers, but Thetis was holding Achilles by the heel when she dipped him. That small part was not protected. The expression "Achilles heel," refers to a small but important weakness.

Eventually Zeus ordered the gods to stay out of the war. When they did, the Trojans began to win. The Greeks desperately needed Achilles. When Achilles' friend was killed in battle, Achilles wanted revenge, so he rejoined the fight.

But Paris, who had also returned to the battle, fired an arrow that Apollo guided to the one spot where Achilles was weak—his heel. The great warrior Achilles died. Soon after, Achilles' son struck Paris with a poisoned arrow, and he died as well.

Despite being nearly mortal, Achilles died during the Trojan War.

The Trojan Horse and the End of the War

With the help of Athena, Odysseus came up with a plan to finally end the war. The Greeks built a huge wooden horse and hid many warriors inside its hollow belly. Then the remaining Greek fighters burned their campsites and sailed away, making it look as if they had given up.

The Trojan Horse was brought inside the walls of Troy.

The horse was left outside the gates of Troy, along with a man named Sinon. When the Trojans discovered the wooden horse, Sinon told them that Athena had become angry with the Greeks. Without her help, they could not win, so they had retreated. Sinon said the horse was a gift for Athena, and if the Trojans destroyed it, they would anger her too.

Not wanting to anger Athena, the Trojans took the horse inside the gates of Troy. That night, while the Trojans slept, the Greek warriors snuck out of the horse and opened the gates to the city. Once the gates were open, the Greek army, which was hiding nearby, stormed inside. They killed nearly everyone inside and burned the city. With that the war was over. With the Greeks' victory, Helen was returned to Sparta. Hera and Athena got their revenge against Paris, and Zeus had accomplished his goal of killing off many humans.

The Literature of the Trojan War

Parts of the Trojan War and its aftermath were recorded in various pieces of literature. Three of the most important were epic poems—Homer's *The Iliad* and *The Odyssey* and Virgil's *The Aeneid*.

The Iliad tells the story of when Achilles refuses to participate in the war after arguing with Agamemnon. Most of *The Iliad* takes place over a short period of time. But essentially the entire story of the Trojan War is contained in *The Iliad*.

The Odyssey tells the story of the Greek hero Odysseus as he journeys back home after the war. He faces many challenges along the way, including battling the one-eyed monster Cyclops and a six-headed serpent called Scylla. He also encounters stormy seas and meets a sorceress who turns his men into pigs.

On his journey home, Odysseus' ship was tossed about by stormy seas. When a thunderbolt struck the ship, only Odysseus survived.

The Aeneid tells the story of Aeneas, a Trojan hero who fled Troy after its downfall. Aeneas overcomes many challenges. He even goes into the Underworld to visit with his dead father. A **prophecy** said that he would found a great new city, so he and his men sail toward Italy. Afterward, according to Virgil, Aeneas arrives in Italy and successfully founds Rome. This city becomes the center of the Roman Empire.

Aeneas (center) journeyed to the Underworld to visit Anchises, his dead father (left). Anchises tells Aeneas of his fate.

prophecy—a prediction

The Greeks Accept Christianity

In 146 BC Greece became part of the Roman Empire. During this time the Romans adopted many parts of Greek culture, including art, philosophy, and literature. They also adopted the Greek myths. However, they substituted the names of Greeks gods with Roman names.

Between the 3rd and 6th centuries, Christianity gradually replaced the traditional Greek religion. But the stories of the Greek gods and goddesses are still widely known today. They have lived on through stories, poems, plays, and art for nearly 3,000 years.

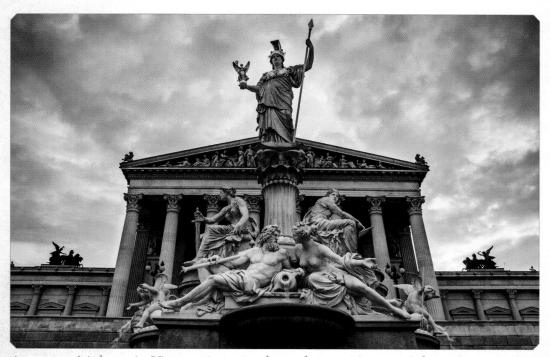

A statue of Athena in Vienna, Austria, shows how widespread the influence of the ancient Greeks still is.

GLOSSARY

architecture (AR-kuh-tek-chuhr)—the design of buildings

city-state (SI-tee STAYT)—a self-governing town and its surrounding territory

democracy (di-MAH-kruh-see)—a form of government in which the citizens can choose their leaders and make decisions by voting

epic poem (EP-ik POH-uhm)—a long story or poem about heroic adventures and great battles

foretell (for-TEL)—to predict something that will happen in the future

fortify (FOR-tuh-fye)—to construct walls or buildings to be used for military defenses

immortal (i-MOR-tuhl)—able to live forever

isolate (EYE-suh-layt)—the condition of being alone

prophecy (PRAH-fuh-see)—a prediction

Titan (TYE-tuhn)—a family of giants in Greek mythology born of Uranus and Gaea and ruling the earth until overthrown by the Olympian gods

trident (TRY-dent)—a long spear with three sharp points at its end

READ MORE

Hoena, Blake. *The Trojan War: An Interactive Mythological Adventure.* You Choose: Ancient Greek Myths. North Mankato, Minn.: Capstone Press, 2017.

Nicolaides, Selene. *Gods, Heroes, and Monsters: Discover the Wonders of the Ancient Greek Myths.* Hauppauge, New York: Barron's, 2016.

Palmer, Erin. *Greek Mythology.* Mythology Marvels. Vero Beach, Fla.: Rourke Educational Media, 2017.

INTERNET SITES

Use FactHound to find Internet sites related to this book.

Visit www.facthound.com

Just type in 9781515796060 and go.

 Check out projects, games and lots more at
www.capstonekids.com

CRITICAL THINKING QUESTIONS

1. The Greek gods were often jealous, angry, and cruel. Why do you think they acted his way? Use details from the text in your answer.

2. Choose two gods or goddesses from the text. In what ways are they similar to each other? In what ways are they different? Use evidence from the text to support your answer.

3. Invent your own god or goddess. What special powers does he or she have? What part of the world does he or she reign over or protect?

INDEX

Achilles, 20, 22, 23, 26
Acropolis of Athens, 5
Aeneas, 20, 28
Agamemnon, 20, 26

Christianity, 29
city-states, 4, 5
creation stories, 8

Euclid, 6

gods and goddesses, 4, 29
　Aphrodite, 11, 18, 20, 22
　Apollo, 10, 12, 16, 20, 23
　Ares, 10
　Artemis, 11, 20
　Athena, 5, 10, 11, 16, 18, 20, 24, 25
　Cronus, 8, 9, 10
　Demeter, 8
　Gaea, 8
　Hades, 11
　Hephaestus, 14
　Hera, 8, 10, 16, 18, 20, 25
　Hestia, 8
　Lyssa, 16
　Poseiden, 8, 11, 20
　Prometheus, 12–13, 14
　Rhea, 8, 10
　Tartarus, 8
　Titans, 8, 9, 12
　Uranus, 8
　Zeus, 8, 9, 10, 11, 12–13, 14, 16, 18, 23, 25
Hector, 20
Helen of Sparta, 18, 20, 25
Heracles' 12 Labors, 16
Hesiod, 8
Hippocrates, 6
Homer, 6

intellectual advancements
　art and architecture, 5, 7, 29
　astronomy, 6
　engineering, 6
　literature, 6, 29
　math and geometry, 6
　medicine, 6
　philosophy, 6, 29
　theater, 6

King Menelaus, 20, 22
King Priam, 18

Mount Olympus, 9, 16
mythical creatures
　Cyclops, 26
　Hydra, 17
　Scylla, 26

Odysseus, 6, 20, 24, 26

Pandora's box, 14
Paris of Troy, 18, 20, 22, 23, 25
Parthenon, 5
Pericles, 5
Pythagoras, 6

River Styx, 22

Sinon, 25

Thetis, 22
Trojan War, 6, 18–25, 26
　literature
　　Aeneid, The, 26, 28
　　Iliad, The, 6, 26
　　Odyssey, The, 6, 26
　Trojan Horse, 24–25

Underworld, 9, 28

Virgil, 26, 28